LETTS GUIDES TO
✧ GARDEN DESIGN ✧

Cottage Garden

LETTS GUIDES TO
✧ GARDEN DESIGN ✧

Cottage Garden

✧ ELISABETH ARTER ✧

CANOPY BOOKS

A Division of Abbeville Publishing Group

NEW YORK LONDON PARIS

First published in the United States in 1993
by Canopy Books, a division of Abbeville Publishing Group,
488 Madison Avenue
New York, NY 10022

First published in the United Kingdom in 1992
by Charles Letts & Co Ltd.
Letts of London House, Parkgate Road
London SW11 4NQ

Edited, designed and produced by Robert Ditchfield Ltd.
Copyright © Robert Ditchfield Ltd 1992.

ISBN 1 – 55859 – 547 – 3

A CIP catalog record for this book is available from the British Library.

ACKNOWLEDGEMENTS
Photographs are reproduced by kind permission of the following:
Robert Ditchfield Ltd. (photographer John Franks): 27, 49 and (photographer Bob
Gibbons) 16, 23, 34, 36, 46; Andrew Lawson: 2, 7, 14, 19, 25, 35, 38, 45; S & O
Matthews: 31, 51; Christine Skelmersdale: 32, 40, 41, 43. All other photographs are
by Diana Saville who would like to thank the owners of the many gardens in which
they were taken, including Barnsley House, Close Farm, Eastgrove Cottage,
Hebbards, Jasmine House, Kingstone Cottages who hold the NCCPG dianthus
collection, Stone House Cottage, Trevi and Well Cottage.

ILLUSTRATIONS
Page 1: Traditional beehive set amongst roses.
Frontispiece: Self-sown poppies with violas and Erysimum 'Bowles' Mauve'.
Page 5: Behind the window, the climbing rose 'Mme Alfred Carrière' is the
background to a jug of old roses.

CONTENTS

ABOVE: *Booted bantams beside* Alchemilla mollis.
OPPOSITE: *Traditional beehive and forcing jars for rhubarb.*

INTRODUCTION

The cottage garden of our dreams has roses and honeysuckle around the door, hollyhocks against the walls, an abundance of old-fashioned flowers and air filled with summer fragrance. It is a romantic idea that may owe more to nostalgia than reality, but it has led to a delightful way of gardening.

Nothing could be better suited to the current longing for a natural life-style than this kind of garden. For, the true 'cottager' makes wildlife welcome, uses only organic materials, grows many native flowers and conserves treasured plants from the past. Many people will choose to grow flowers and foliage only, but there should also be a place for herbs, fruit and vegetables and, for those determined to be true to tradition and move nearer self-sufficiency, a few hives of bees, some poultry – and, perhaps, a pig fattening in a sty.

In keeping with a simple life-style, this is an economical way to garden for most cottage plants are fully hardy and any replacements can be raised from seed or cuttings. Flowers that have sometimes survived for centuries are mostly sturdy individuals that need no costly chemical care to keep them healthy; and, anyway, pest and disease problems are fewer when many different kinds of plant are intermingled rather than when big blocks of one type are grown. If they are put in close together, plants also support one another, or can be propped up by twiggy sticks cut off during winter pruning. Other vegetable refuse may go on the compost heap; whilst scrap materials can be used to make paths and seats or turned into containers for plants near the house. Even rain water can be saved if it is collected in butts and here is another way in which the modern gardener can assist with conservation. Nothing should be wasted and every inch of space utilized.

A Natural Garden

There is no place for a lawn or modern paved patio for sitting out in a true cottage garden, but there are always a few seats against the walls or sheltered by arbours covered in climbing plants. Paths are functional and lead directly from one part to another, with their edges softened by the overflowing growth on either side. Everything looks as though it has grown naturally; flowering plants are never regimented into straight lines, nor are there any bare patches of earth, for something new goes into the space immediately it becomes available.

If you plant generously and encourage self-seeding, a cottage garden should be a riot of colour, but in the soft muted shades that blend harmoniously rather than in the harsh tones of so many modern roses and bedding plants. The air should be filled with the perfume of flowers and foliage, with the humming of bees and with butterflies flitting from bloom to bloom.

Above all a true cottage garden is a friendly place that makes you feel welcome when you walk in the gate and that you can tell is tended with affectionate care and filled with favourite plants. Many of them hold memories for the gardener and will have been grown from bits and pieces that have been offered from other equally loved gardens, for the owners are as generous with gifts to one another as with their planting.

Tall yellow spires of Asphodeline lutea among purple geraniums.

THE HISTORY OF COTTAGE GARDENS

When meat was often in short supply in medieval times, vegetables had to be a main part of the diet for poorer people. In cottage gardens, it was usual to grow peas and beans to dry for winter, root crops, leeks, onions and cabbages. Many pot herbs were planted for flavouring to disguise the poor quality of the food and the fact that it was often far from fresh. Other herbs were grown to ward off witchcraft and evil spirits, to make remedies, strew on floors and use for dyes.

In England, the range of plants increased after the Dissolution of the Monasteries in the sixteenth century, as villagers who were cut off from the herbal medicines supplied by the monks, began to grow more of their own. No doubt, they helped themselves to plants that were growing in the deserted monastery gardens, probably acquiring, too, some of the Madonna lilies and white roses that had long been grown for church decoration.

Until then the only flowers to be included, other than those of such cheery herbs as the gay orange pot marigold, were probably extra pretty or out-of-the-ordinary specimens of wild plants dug up from the surrounding countryside, such as the double form of the lesser celandine (Ranunculus ficaria).

Later, no doubt, many cuttings and layered pieces of cultivated plants came to cottage gardens from the large gardens of the gentry where so many sons and daughters found work in the house or outside. This would have continued to happen as more and more exciting new discoveries were introduced from distant lands by plant hunters.

There was probably little fruit in early cottage gardens, the variety increasing as orchards were planted, and when numerous different kinds were introduced into the kitchen gardens of the big houses. Here many luxury fruits needed the shelter of a warm wall or protection by glass, but those grown by humbler people were hardy varieties.

More new flowers came to cottage gardens with the arrival of the Huguenots and other refugees. For they brought a love of the so-called florist's blooms, such as auriculas and laced pinks, which were hybridized to improve the size and shape and became popular for competition growing.

Many of the old-fashioned plants we think of today as cottage flowers are probably descended from those thrown out from the gardens of the gentry in the late eighteenth century when 'Capability' Brown destroyed many acres of ornamental flower beds to make landscaped parks with sweeping vistas of grass, water and trees. You can imagine the working people bearing home unwanted plants in triumph to their own humble plots.

In the really old days flowers would not have been grown in borders on their own, but mingled among the culinary plants – a practice you can still see in some of the old cottage gardens that are even now in existence. Tall hollyhocks might have leant on the branch of an apple tree, climbing roses be tied to the clothes posts that held up the washing line, pansies would have grown among the gooseberry bushes and scented flowers made an edging for the vegetable plot. Herbs were much used as edgings also, being grown by paths and near the kitchen door.

Cottage gardens, however small, were usually enclosed by hedges; these were often of hawthorn, or 'quick', that could be dug up as small plants from the surrounding countryside and would very soon grow into a dense prickly barrier. Sometimes the slower-growing evergreen holly or yew might be used, or other native deciduous shrubs and trees would be mixed with the hawthorn. Over the years ivy often became intertwined with the thorn to give a hedge that provided food and shelter for small wild creatures.

The laced pink 'Old Dutch' with violas, cowslips and fennel.

Modern Cottage Gardens

A s time went on and the labouring classes became less impoverished, flowers and food crops became more separated and it was usual for the husband to grow the vegetables in neat rows in one part of the garden and to care for the fruit trees and bushes, while his wife grew a mixed medley of flowers and shrubs in gay abandon in another. She did not trust him to weed among her plants lest some treasure was pulled out by mistake, and he grumbled good-naturedly about the untidiness of her patch.

Over the past couple of hundred years there has been also a trend for those from the upper and middle classes to adopt a simple life that was close to nature and the modern idea of cottage gardening has more to do with this than with the labourers who chose what to grow and how to grow it from necessity.

Late last century William Robinson, author of that classic of gardening literature, *The English Flower Garden*, wrote that "among

ABOVE: *Cottage topiary in yew, painstakingly trimmed into fantastic birds on pillars.*

LEFT: *The sunset colours of the cottage garden at Sissinghurst Castle – dahlias, hemerocallis, roses and verbascum.*

things made by man nothing is prettier than an English cottage garden", and waged a long battle against the artificially formal style of bedding-out used so much in many Victorian gardens. Gertrude Jekyll liked his ideas and wrote of "learning much from the little cottage gardens that help to make our English waysides the pret-

tiest in the temperate world". The world-famous garden at Sissinghurst Castle, Kent, created by Vita Sackville-West and her husband Sir Harold Nicolson, earlier this century was much inspired by these two great gardeners. Hidcote Manor Garden in Gloucestershire, created by the American Lawrence Johnston a few decades earlier, has other good examples of 'cottage' planting.

But it was Margery Fish and the garden she made and wrote about at East Lambrook Manor in Somerset who revived the greatest interest in "the simple steadfast qualities" of cottage flowers.

She was concerned that they might be lost and would be delighted to see the growing enthusiasm for these old treasures today.

Modern cottage gardeners have been much influenced also by Helen Allingham and other romantic nineteenth century artists who have given us an idealized view of rural contentment with their paintings of 'chocolate box' cottages surrounded by a luxuriant wealth of pretty flowers, blended naturally with fruit and vegetables. This may not be true to life, but gives a good idea of the type of plants most suited to this style of gardening.

11

PLANTS FROM THE PAST

O ne of the joys of a cottage garden is that it is the ideal place for plants that have been grown and loved for centuries, but which do not blend into the usual modern layout. In fact, some of these old treasures were at risk of being lost to cultivation until rescued by new enthusiasts for this homely style. It only needs one plant lover to preserve a rarity, propagate from it and share resulting plants with friends to conserve a bit of our floral heritage.

One plant that was thought to have been lost is the double form of the red campion (*Silene dioica*), now available from a number of nurseries. Double flowers were much loved in the old days and other wild plants whose double forms were cultivated include the pale mauve lady's smock (*Cardamine pratensis*), bright blue meadow cranesbill (*Geranium pratense*) and golden-yellow marsh marigold (*Caltha palustris*).

Plant oddities appealed to people in the past and an example that is still grown today is the curious hen and chicken daisy; this looks just like a common wild daisy (*Bellis perennis*) except that a ring of tiny flowers grows out from the main bloom. Another is the green rose plantain, a strange form of the wild greater plantain (*Plantago major*) in which the normal slim flower spike is replaced by a rosette that at its best resembles a green cabbage rose.

The snowdrop (*Galanthus nivalis*) whose dainty white flowers are one of the first harbingers of spring has been with us so long that no one seems sure whether it is a native or if wild plants are all that remain of some long vanished cottage garden.

You can tell that a flower has been grown

Geranium pratense 'Flore Pleno', treasured for centuries for its double flowers.

Lychnis coronaria *was grown in the fourteenth century. It self-seeds lightly.*

since way back in the past if it has a number of common names or has been associated with the Virgin Mary. Very early in spring, lungwort (*Pulmonaria officinalis*) opens its pink and blue flowers that have earned it the names Joseph and Mary and soldiers and sailors. White spots on the green leaves that led to the name spotted dog were said to come from spilt drops of the Virgin's milk and in the Doctrine of Signatures were thought to suggest the plant could cure lung disease – hence the commonest name.

The rose campion (*Lychnis coronaria*) with furry silver leaves and branching stems topped by single magenta blooms was grown as early as the fourteenth century and was known also as rose of Mary and Christ's eye. A short-lived perennial, easy to raise from seed, it is well suited to the cottage garden.

The shrubby southernwood (*Artemesia abrotanum*) was grown in the old days for the strong aroma of the feathery foliage that, when gathered and brought indoors, was thought to help ward off infection and deter the clothes moth. In the garden it is still said to prevent aphis on nearby roses and cabbage-white butterfly attack on greenstuff. There is a romantic notion that the common name of lad's love was given because sprigs were so often included in nosegays for country sweethearts, but it is more likely this refers to the use of the herb to promote growth of the beard and hair.

Many members of the pink family (Dianthus) were grown in the old days, and one that dates back to antiquity is the biennial sweet william (*D. barbatus*). It was once called London pride, but that name has now been used for *Saxifraga* × *urbium* for over two hundred years.

13

Quintessential cottage plants: pink lupins with delphiniums and Oriental poppies.

MODERN PLANTS IN AN OLD TRADITION

The cottage garden is in an old tradition, but that does not mean it should become a museum filled only with plants from way back in the past. Instead it should incorporate also the best of those new introductions which are in keeping with the style, and blend happily with our old treasures.

Double forms of the wild primrose (*Primula vulgaris*) were great favourites in Tudor times and some varieties have survived down the years, but need tender care to grow well. However, recent years have seen the introduction of some exciting new varieties and the twentieth century cottager will find it easier to grow such pretty primroses as the lilac 'Easter Bonnet', rosy-red 'April Rose' and white-rimmed purple 'Miss Indigo'.

Russell Lupins were not exhibited for the first time at a Royal Horticultural Society show until 1937, yet fit so well into a cottage garden that they are often assumed to date back very much further. Dwarf strains such as 'Lulu' are even newer, but can be better in a garden exposed to strong winds.

The sweet pea first came to Britain from its native Sicily three hundred years ago, but it was not until early this century that the first of the Spencer type commonly grown today was introduced. The Old-Fashioned Mixture offered by most seedsmen may have the richest scent, but there is no doubt that all kinds of sweet pea look appropriate alongside other cottage flowers. Grow them in a hedge-style to climb up tall bushy sticks for the best effect.

A drawback to many of the old roses was that they bloomed only at midsummer and came just in shades of pink, crimson and white. English roses bred by David Austin are a new race that combine the recurrent flowering and wider colour range of modern Hybrid Teas and Floribundas with the characteristic flower formation and charm of the old roses. Their growth is more natural and bushy than that of a Hybrid Tea and all are deliciously fragrant. New varieties come out each year and among the best are the pink 'Mary Rose', yellow 'Graham Thomas', rich crimson 'The Prince' and apricot-blush 'Perdita'.

Allwoodii pinks raised in the 1920s by the Allwood Brothers from a cross between a perpetual carnation and the white garden pink, 'Old Fringed', are faster growing, truly hardy, bloom several times in a season and fit into a cottage garden nearly as well as the old pinks that date back much further. 'Doris' which is salmon-pink with a darker centre is the most widely grown.

Some of the recent novelties from the leading seed houses are very much in the old tradition. Carnation 'Peach Delight' makes fine clumps of beautifully scented blooms; the 'Angel's Blush' form of rose campion (*Lychnis coronaria*) has white flowers with pink centres that spread with age and the 'Indian Prince' form of calendula which is glowing orange with a mahogany reverse is also a joy to grow as an annual.

'Cymbeline', one of the most heavily scented of the English roses which flower recurrently.

Earlier this century there was a trend for bigger brighter blooms, but happily the fashion has now changed in favour of softer colours and smaller flowers. Some varieties of the double daisy (*Bellis perennis*) looked like small dahlias, but now we can enjoy the petite pink, red or white 'Double Carpet' and we can grow the neat blue 'Baby Lucia' or yellow 'Baby Franjo' violas instead of the huge pansies of a generation or so ago which can look rather overblown in comparison.

PLANNING AND PLANTING

The cottage style suits every size of garden in town or country and although it seems more in keeping with an older property, it can look equally good with a modern home so long as planting is lavish and lots of climbers are used to cover up quickly the stark bare look of a new building.

With a brand new home, or one recently converted or restored, you may have the chance to work on a completely clean canvas once the builder's rubble and overgrown weeds have been cleared. But it is far more likely you will be starting with an established garden, or the remains of a derelict plot which goes with many older cottages.

If you take over a cottage that had been restored by previous owners, any old planting will probably have been ripped out and replaced by a lawn surrounded by a Leyland cypress hedge plus perhaps a few dwarf conifers and spaces for some summer bedding plants. This looks awful in a rural setting, but seems the number-one choice for people who are faced with a bit of land and have little idea how to garden. You can change this kind of scheme without difficulty. It is simple to dig up a large expanse of lawn and go over to a new design and you can quite easily keep some of the

The old rambler rose, 'Mme d'Arbley', drapes an apple tree.

grass mown and tidy while you gradually make the plant beds and borders.

With an established garden, however derelict, you need to move more slowly and wait for an entire growing season to discover what is there already. Cutting long weeds may reveal old brick paths, or roses and shrubs which are worth pruning carefully to ensure they have a new lease of life. You may also discover many spring bulbs and perennials as they come up.

Don't cut down any fruit trees until they have had a chance to crop once and,

even if the apples, pears or plums they bear are of poor quality, the trees can offer support for climbing plants and shade for early small bulbs or woodland plants. Trees that do have to come down may provide wood to make log seats or slim branches to make tripods for supporting old roses and twiggy sticks to make a sweet pea hedge. Hidden among the undergrowth you may also find old sinks, chimney pots and junk which might be suitable for conversion into plant containers. Beware of throwing anything away that could be useful.

A town cottage garden, packed with plants. The rose 'Climbing Iceberg' twines round a pillar.

Sitting Out

A priority in any garden is a sitting-out area that will need some shade in summer, but is sheltered and sunny for most of the year. Brick pavers or crazy paving are more suitable for a cottage garden than the large regularly-shaped paving stones used for the modern patio. The generous use of climbing plants and containers overflowing with flowers and foliage will soon give the area an established look. Fill some of the crevices between the paving with soil or old potting compost and sow a few pinches of creeping thyme seed among it; this is one of the finest aromatic carpeting plants, and will soften the look of the stone and give off a rich perfume when trodden. Next summer some of your self-seeders will fill other crevices to give a natural old-world look to a terrace or patio.

Lawn

A lawn is not in keeping with the true cottage garden tradition, but a small area of turf surrounded by brimful beds of bloom need not spoil the style. To avoid the effort of edging and to allow for the luxuriant growth of plants, lay one row of paving stones between a lawn and its adjoining borders. You can often produce a very satisfactory turf if you mow the existing grass and weeds regularly, provided the site has an even surface. But it is usually better to start with the ground worked down to a smooth level finish; you can then sow lawn seed in early spring or late summer, or lay turves, ideally in early autumn. Land dug over and manured in winter, then used for a 'cleaning' crop of potatoes will be weed-free and well-prepared for making a lawn.

17

Panorama of a cottage garden, intensively planted with hardy perennials.

Site Preparation

Before anything goes in, you need to dig the site over thoroughly, working in plenty of organic material and taking care to remove all perennial weed roots. A good way of clearing an area overrun with hard-to-clear weeds is to smother them with a mulch of old carpet, lino or stout plastic sacks for several months. The alternative is to use a blanket weedkiller and leave land vacant for two or three months before planting. Nothing is so good as deep and thorough digging of the site for a new border, but a great deal of time and effort can be saved by using modern machinery. Hire a strimmer to clear rubbish and a powered cultivator to dig over the site. Work in generous amounts of well-rotted organic matter, for even soil that looks a good rich dark colour may be impoverished.

Design

A cottage garden should look as though it evolved naturally, with no planning, but there has to be some idea of a design before you plant. Start with the bare bones of the garden, deciding where paths, shed or other outbuildings, arbour or summerhouse, trees and large shrubs are to go. Hedges, fences and paths should follow straight lines to balance the seemingly haphazard way of planting. There is a modern fashion for vegetables and flowers to be mixed together, but though the true cottager grows both, culinary plants are better alone in an open sunny site, with a wide edging of herbs, soft fruit, or scented flowers between them and the path. In a larger garden, fruit trees can be planted in a small orchard, but when just a few are grown they can be under-planted with spring bulbs and those old perennial plants that like the dappled shade found under deciduous trees. A row of well-spaced taller old roses growing over tripods of rustic poles looks splendid along the centre of a border and climbing roses can clamber over a rustic frame at the back.

Oriental poppies, geraniums and campanulas form a close tapestry on the ground.

A cottage should be surrounded by a patchwork of perennial planting aimed at giving colour all year, with different plants merging into one another in random fashion or allowed to self-seed and pop up in unexpected places. Annual flowers that last for just the one season are a wise choice for any new garden, because they make a quick show that can be enjoyed while you are planning where any longerterm planting should go.

Use some evergreen shrubs surrounded by hellebores, early small bulbs and perennials that retain their leaves through the cold months for winter interest. Grow the primrose family, first of the border flowers, biennials and bulbs as mainstay of the spring display. Roses, perennials and annuals in abundance will give a summer show and late perennials and plants with pretty seed heads, fruits, or leaf colours will keep it going through autumn.

19

RIGHT: *Peonies can be propagated by division in autumn.*

STOCKING THE GARDEN

With the increasing interest in old-fashioned plants it is far easier than it was a few years ago to find cottage garden plants on sale in nurseries and garden centres, the most interesting finds usually coming from smaller specialist firms. There are some very good named varieties, and some splendid modern hybrids to grow in your borders, but many old favourites have never been given the accolade of a varietal name.

There should be little need to buy if you follow tradition, for surplus plants and propagating material have always been passed on from garden to garden and from generation to generation. Elderly gardeners are often very willing to give plant material to newcomers to the hobby and by accepting pieces from them you may conserve plants not available commercially. There is often a complaint that modern varieties of Christmas rose (*Helleborus niger*) are reluctant to bloom for the festive season. I was told by an octogenarian gardener, whose plants flower reliably early, that newer forms bloom later than old ones; her plants had been given to her many years ago by a ninety-year-old cottager.

Propagation

There are many valuable modern aids to propagation and you will benefit from the use of a heated propagator and a greenhouse, but for a simple cottage garden you can rely on using windowsills indoors for early warmth and a cold frame in the open. This can be made from an old fully glazed window and planks of wood for the sides, or even from a pane of glass and a bottomless wooden box. Of course, seeds of many hardy plants will germinate and hardwood cuttings root successfully in open ground.

Seed

The majority of hardy annual flowers can be started from seed. They can be sown where they are intended to flower, in an open sunny position on well-drained soil in early spring. Your timing depends not so much on the calendar, more on the condition of the soil: it should have dried out and warmed up enough to be raked into a fine tilth. The hardiest annuals, such as larkspur, calendula, cornflower and eschscholzia, can also be sown at the end of summer and this produces the earliest blooms and strongest plants the following year. Once established these plants will ripen and shed seeds to give young plants year after year with little further need for sowing, so long as dead-heading is not carried out too efficiently.

An entire border of hardy annuals can look lovely and is ideal in a new garden while longer-term plants are being propagated. But more often you want just a few plants to fill gaps among perennials. There can be problems with young seedlings being smothered by neighbouring plants or eaten by slugs and snails if you sow *in situ*. Better results will usually come from sowing seed in a special bed, and you can transplant the seedlings when they are good-sized young plants. Or you can start the hardies along with the half-hardy annuals that need the protection of glass, and sometimes the warmth of a windowsill indoors, to germinate well.

Border of half-hardy annuals, its charm due to the intermingling of colours and species. They are sown early under glass.

Under cover, sow the seed in yoghurt cartons or small pots, filled with damp vermiculite; cover the pots with plastic or glass and stand them in a warm spot until the first seedlings emerge. The pots should then be uncovered, moved to a cooler place and the seedlings pricked out into individual pots, wooden or plastic seed trays or planting strips as soon as they are large enough to handle. Grow them on and gradually harden them off before planting out; the half-hardies will need protection at night until any risk of frost is past.

A large number of cottage garden plants will self-seed to provide a new generation, but there is also the chance for you to collect ripe seeds to sow yourself. This gives you the opportunity to preserve seed from selected heads of the strongest plants or most beautifully coloured and it is the way in which improved strains have been produced down the years. It was, for example, the way in which the Revd W. Wilks of Shirley bred the beautiful Shirley poppies late last century from just one wild red poppy with white edged petals.

Wait until the chosen seed head is just ripe; then on a dry day cover it with a paper bag, cut the stem and hang it up to dry in the bag in a warm airy shed. Allow a week or so and you will find seeds have fallen out ready to be sown right away or stored in small clearly labelled paper packets in a cool dry place for sowing the next spring.

Cuttings

Many roses and woody plants can be raised from hardwood cuttings taken in early autumn from well-ripened healthy stems of the current season's growth. Each one should be cut through (straight across) just below a leaf joint at the bottom, and given a sloping cut above a leaf joint at the top. The size of each will vary with the plant, but 10in/25cm is a good average length. Clearly labelled and inserted firmly to half their depth in a corner of the garden, the cuttings should produce rooted plants for moving to permanent positions the next autumn. Regular watering in dry weather in the spring is vital to ensure good rooting.

Many herbs, roses, shrubs and woody plants can be raised from half-ripe cuttings taken in mid to late summer from shoots of the current season's growth that are beginning to mature. You may need to cut away the softest tip growth and usually the cutting will be no more than half the length of a hardwood one taken later in the

ABOVE: The suckering rose 'William's Double Yellow' amongst thrift.

LEFT: In this border of hostas, mallow and campanulas, note how seed-heads (on the right) have been left to ripen.

fifty/fifty mix of peat and sand or perlite. Stand this pot in a warm, but shaded place and keep it damp. Depending on the species, rooting may take from one to several months. Once new growth starts from the top of a cutting it should be ready to move on to a nursery bed in the open ground or to an individual pot to be kept in the cold frame through winter.

Layers

Roots will form on the shoots of many woody plants if they are in contact with the soil and, to assist

season. It can be cut through at the bottom, or pulled away from the main shoot with a small heel of bark, which will need trimming with a sharp knife before the cutting is inserted. A row of these cuttings can go in the open garden, but it is better to put them in a cold frame, or insert a number around the sides of a pot filled with a

this, you can peg down some shoots with bits of bent wire. Sometimes roots can be encouraged to form if the stem is partly cut in advance. Mounding a bit of leafmould or pulverized bark around the base of a woody plant, such as thyme, also induces roots to form.

Irishmen's cuttings (where stems are cut away from the parent plant with a bit of root already forming at the base), suckers from plants with running roots, and sections from clump-forming hardy perennials that have been split up are other trouble-free and reliable ways of making one plant into a number of others.

23

PATHS, WALLS AND FENCES

Straight, serviceable paths suit the very informal planting of a cottage garden. At the front the path should go directly from the gate to the door and, at the rear, from the back door to the shed, compost heap, arbour, hen-house or any other place that will be visited almost daily. Because the plants will be encouraged to spill over on either side, the main paths should be 3 – 4ft/1-1.2m wide and made of materials that will allow them to be used in all weathers.

BELOW: *Pinks, the prostrate Hebe 'Carl Teschner' and* Penstemon glaber *spread over a gravel path in colourful profusion.*

Materials for Paths

Stone or frost-resistant brick makes a very attractive path, but can be costly. Crazy paving will soon mellow if you leave crevices between the pieces for mat-forming plants. Brick rubble and broken tiles from work on the cottage, or stones picked out when you dig the garden, will all make a good firm and free-draining base for a path if well compacted. A topping of gravel will provide a path for little cost.

Narrow access paths which enable you to dead-head or cut flowers, gather herbs and harvest fruit or vegetables can be made from pieces of broken paving slabs. Our you can build them out of thick slices cut from trunks of trees, demolished perhaps while clearing the garden, setting them into the ground in stepping-stone fashion. Bark chippings, shredded woody prunings or sawdust are good materials for temporary paths that may be moved after a few seasons as the garden design evolves.

Planting outside as well as within the cottage garden: Clematis montana rubens *smothers iron railings.*

Walls

Dry stone walls look delightful with a cottage, particularly in areas where they are a feature of the countryside. As they are built, pockets of soil can be planted with small ferns on the shady side and with stonecrops, houseleeks and easy alpines on the top and sunny sides. You may be able to collect flints or other local stones from farmland, with permission from landowners glad to be rid of them. Old weathered bricks make attractive walls, especially if you leave a few small pockets for planting among the mortar.

Fences

The materials used for fences will depend on the locality and your budget. Stakes and wire netting or galvanized chain-link are inexpensive and will quickly enclose a back garden to define the boundary, keep out intruders and keep in pets and toddlers. Plant honeysuckle, virginia creeper, rambler roses and other vigorous climbers to grow up and over the fence and after a few years it can look most pleasing. Chestnut paling and post-and-rail fences are both very suitable for rural back gardens. Where higher fences or those that give more privacy and shelter are needed, featherboard panels are the strongest available, but cost nearly twice as much as the more popular interwoven panels. Featherboarding looks almost as good as a wall around a small enclosed courtyard garden and makes a fine background for less vigorous climbers or wall-trained fruit.

In the front a wooden gate looks best with a cottage whether the garden is surrounded by hedge, wall, or fence. A picket fence can look lovely painted white, with red valerian (*Centranthus ruber*) and other free-and-easy plants growing through from the garden, but regular maintenance is time-consuming and costly; wood treated with timber preservative is a better choice for an elderly gardener or one with little time and a low budget. Do leave a narrow strip of land outside the fence to fill with plants for passers-by to enjoy.

25

Rustic arches look perfect in a cottage garden, but nylon-coated steel soon blends in once climbers have got going. Plant one on each side, choosing two that will flower at different times – perhaps a rose for mid-summer colour and a large-flowered clematis to follow.

If you are going to stay in one place for years there is the chance to create a living arch from two beeches or yews clipped to form up-rights and then trained to grow into one another at the top. Time and patience will be rewarded by the all-year beauty of the mature archway.

Arbours

Make a rustic arbour facing the sun with top, back and sides of rough poles and a seat fashioned from stout planks. Plant scented climbers to grow up and hide the framework, and creeping thyme and other aromatics among bricks or paving in the path leading to it.

A seat under a planted arch against the sunny side of a shed, high fence or hedge will make a warm bower for you to sit in for much of the year. By contrast a seat or a table and chairs positioned beneath several linked arches, festooned with climbers, will make a cool shaded summer retreat.

ARCHWAYS, SEATS AND BUILDINGS

The modern fashion for garden archways suits the old cottage style admirably, so long as these structures are simple and used as plant supports rather than ornaments. How welcoming is the garden viewed through a flower-covered archway over the front gate, or the cottage with a rustic arch smothered in roses or honeysuckle, taking the place of a porch to the front door. An arch over a main path should not be less than 8ft/2.5m high to allow room to walk underneath without stooping when it is covered by plant growth. It also needs to be sited a bit back from the path edge on either side to avoid plants narrowing the walking space.

The building is smothered in swags of golden ivy and Lathyrus latifolius.

Seats

*E*very cottage garden must have a few seats, mainly against warm walls or in sunny sheltered spots. The simpler the seat the more it is in character. You can make a wooden seat to encircle a tree-trunk or you could turn sections from a fallen tree into log seats and stand one against the cottage wall.

Buildings

*A*n old cottage may have sufficient outbuildings made of the same materials; if not, any you put up will look in keeping if walls and roofs match. But, as costs often rule this out, you will probably have to compromise. Timber generally blends in more readily than plastic or metal but, whatever material is chosen, the secret of blending buildings into the landscape is to plant climbers against the walls, using some of those like *Clematis montana* that are vigorous enough to go right over the roof.

A shed near the end of the garden is sensible if you have a long or sloping plot, for it saves many journeys to and from the house for tools and sundries. Site the shed to hide eyesores such as the compost heap in your own and neighbouring gardens. Train fruit on its walls and grow a row of tomatoes against a sunny side.

A really basic shelter made from four stout poles supporting a lean-to roof against a wall will serve well for the log store that is vital if you have a wood-burning stove. Site the coal bunker, the central-heating oil store, or any other necessary but unlovely object, out of view of your windows, or hidden by a screen of planted trellis or hedge. This prevents the garden being spoilt by an ugly eyesore.

Double hedges; the plants are colour-coordinated each side of the inner division.

HEDGES

It is traditional for the cottage garden to be enclosed by a hedge and this should be neatly clipped to contrast with the spilling lush growth of the flower beds. Informal flowering hedges, in the modern manner, are less suited to backing beds in this kind of garden.

Hawthorn (*Crataegus monogyna*), also called quickthorn or may, has probably been used for hedging longer than any other plant. It is quick and easy to establish, grows on most soils, in cold and warm areas, and is tolerant of cutting and the layering which has been carried out in rural areas for centuries to prevent hedges becoming too large or developing gaps at ground level. The best results come from planting small hawthorns at 1ft/30cm apart and, as with most hedges, a temporary stake and netting fence will be needed for the first few years.

An old and overgrown hawthorn hedge can usually be brought back into shape if you cut one side back very hard in late winter one year. After that has recovered and made new growth, you treat the other side to equally drastic surgery the following winter.

Sometimes other woody plants, such as dog rose, elder, sloe, wayfaring tree, dogwood and holly, are put in with the hawthorn, but in older mixed hedges they have often grown from seeds brought there by the wind or birds. As a general rule it is said that one additional woody species is added every century and that a hedge containing ten different plants dates back a thousand years.

Beech (*Fagus sylvatica*) is a splendid deciduous hedging plant, its russet leaves hanging on the tree through much of the winter. It grows in most soils and will withstand and filter wind far better than any fence. Again the best results come from planting the young trees closely and when small.

Yew (*Taxus baccata*) makes a very good clipped evergreen hedge that is a lovely dark background to colourful flower borders and is not as slow-growing as is often believed. The foliage is poisonous to livestock and so should not be chosen for a garden next to pastureland. An old and overgrown yew hedge can be renovated in the same way as hawthorn, but do the job in mid-spring.

Holly (*Ilex aquifolium*) is slow to grow away and takes some years to make a hedge, but once established is very hardy, suitable for any soil, for town or country and, being evergreen, looks good all year. The seventeenth-century diarist, John Evelyn, wrote of the glorious sight of the impregnable 400 feet long holly hedge in his Thames-side garden. You sometimes see a holly tree growing up out of a mixed hedge and that is because, in the past, country people believed it unlucky to cut the evergreen except at Christmas. Follow the tradition by planting a holly among a mixed, mainly hawthorn hedge, but leave the evergreen unclipped.

Grow a low hedge to separate different parts of the garden, or to edge a drive or

Low box edging; with Hemerocallis 'Whichford' and Clematis 'Victoria'.

path, of old English lavender (*Lavandula angustifolia*) with aromatic silvery foliage and spikes of mauve bloom loved by bees and butterflies; but be prepared for it to grow to a yard (metre) high and across. Cotton lavender (*Santolina chamaecyparis-*

sus) has silvery filigree foliage and golden button blooms, is neater in habit and, like lavender, can be started in situ from cuttings. Use the evergreen edging box *Buxus sempervirens* 'Suffru-ticosa' where a neat un-clipped hedge is needed.

Peony-flowered annual poppies with eryngium.

ANNUALS

Annual flowers in the cottage garden tradition are mainly the hardy kinds that are easy to raise and will often self-seed, so there is no need to sow them anew each year. They are usually more softly coloured than many modern forms with their brash tones, but whereas these may give colour over several months, the old kinds tend to run to seed fairly quickly even if dead-headed regularly. Older annuals generally make taller, bushier plants that may need supporting with a few twiggy sticks.

A truly dwarf hardy annual is the Virginian stock (*Malcolmia maritima*), which is good for sowing in paving crevices and has tiny single flowers of red, lilac, yellow and white. To keep it going all summer, it is best to sow several batches of seed. Often treated as a half-hardy, sweet alyssum (*Lobularia maritima*) is popular for edging bedding schemes, but suitable too for sowing among paving. Originally white, it now has varieties in several colours.

In contrast to these tinies there is the giant single annual sunflower (*Helianthus annus*) with huge round blooms on stems reaching up to the sky. It is best grown against a wall.

Some of the cornfield annuals have been grown in gardens so long that their wild beginnings are seldom remembered. There is the cornflower itself (*Centaurea cyanus*), quite tall and a deep blue in the oldest and most attractive varieties; the Shirley poppy

Glorious annual tapestry of larkspur, marigolds, nasturtium, godetia and sweet peas.

(*Papaver rhoeas*) bred from the red field poppy, but with a pretty colour range, double and single forms and far less promiscuous habit; and corn cockle (*Agrostemma githago* '*Milas*') whose bright pink flowers are larger and showier than those of the species offered among wild flower seeds.

The peony-flowered poppy (*Papaver somniferum*) has been bred from the opium poppy native to Asia and was originally single, though doubles have been grown since the seventeenth century. Huge blooms on quite tall plants with glaucous foliage precede showy seed heads. Another old annual that is a prolific self-seeder is love-in-a-mist (*Nigella damascena*), with pretty blue flowers in the older 'Miss Jekyll' variety, set among feathery bracts and foliage. Its seed heads are showy enough for indoor vases. The newer 'Persian

Jewels' variety comes in mixed colours.

The tall single climbing nasturtium (*Tropaeolum majus*) is the old form that best fits a cottage garden and is lovely when allowed to clamber up and smother a hawthorn hedge with gay red and yellow bloom from midsummer until autumn frosts. Or you can grow the plants up netting or strings to add colour to the side of a new shed.

The sweet pea (*Lathyrus odoratus*) looks better growing up tall bushy sticks in a hedge-style and will flower over the longest period if fragrant blooms are picked regularly.

Other old annuals for a cottage garden include the richly-scented mignonette, cornflower-like sweet sultan, bright, breezy eschscholzia, quick-growing candytuft, tall slim larkspur and love-lies-bleeding with long drooping crimson blooms.

BIENNIALS

The true biennials that complete their life-cycle in two growing seasons and those short-lived perennials that we normally discard after one flowering are both easy-going types of plants, well-suited to the cottage garden. Whilst most of them have been grown for a very long time, some are the result of modern breeding yet fit into this happy-go-lucky style of gardening perfectly.

New Plants in the Old Style

Among these comparative newcomers are the Russell Lupins, with tall spikes of pea-type blooms in a range of lovely colours; the F1 Hybrid Champagne Bubble strain of Iceland Poppy (*Papaver nudicaule*) that is a great improvement on older varieties; and the Excelsior Hybrid foxgloves that come in several good pastel colours, have florets all round the stems and are taller than the rosy-mauve *Digitalis purpurea* which is so good in shadier parts of the garden.

There are many varieties of the pansy (*Viola tricolor*). Despite the introduction of fresh blood from other species, these have been bred mainly from the wild heartsease that grows in farm fields. The fashion today has reverted in favour of these small-flowered pansies, but whether you go for the miniature blue 'Baby Lucia', the huge blooms of Majestic Giants, or prefer something midway in size like the very hardy mixed Floral Dance, they will look right by a cottage.

For Fragrance

The richly-scented wallflower is one of several old plants once known as gilly-flowers. The best results come from growing good strong plants in a nursery-bed from a late spring sowing and then planting them out in a sunny spot on dryish soil where the roots won't be vulnerable to winter frost. They are ideal for narrow beds or containers at the foot

Violas and Ornithogalum umbellatum.

of a sunny house wall. Choose the taller, older varieties such as 'Blood Red', 'Cloth of Gold' and 'Fire King' and the more compact 'Mixed Bedder' or its individual shades.

The sweet william (*Dianthus barbatus*), with flat heads of scented flowers on stiff stems which are ideal for cutting, helps fill the gap between the spring bedding and bulbs and the first of the summer perennials and roses. It is easy from an outdoor sowing and the wise gardener collects seed from ripe heads each year to sow next spring and bloom two years on. 'Giant Auricula Eyed Mixed' is a good strain and 'Crimson Velvet' good if you prefer just one colour.

Once you have raised sweet rocket (*Hesperis matronalis*) from seed one year it will usually self-seed enough to keep a supply going for years, but though you might start off with both mauve and white plants, the white tend to take over after a time. The branching plants of four-petalled flowers will fill the whole garden with their rich fragrance on early summer evenings. There is a double mauve form which was once popular, but this is now a choice rarity.

Bedding

The forget-me-not (myosotis) has been much used for formal spring bedding, but

Sweet William, one of the most scented of biennials, will tolerate a little shade whilst preferring sun.

is equally valuable for planting in small groups at the front of a mixed border, as an underplanting for later-flowering roses and for filling any small spaces that call for a bit of extra spring colour. Buy seed of a good variety like 'Royal Blue', pull up the best plants when flowers are done, and lay them down in an odd corner of the garden. When small seedlings develop, move these to a nursery bed where they can grow on until they are planted out in their flowering positions in autumn.

The double daisy (*Bellis perennis*) is splendid, too, for filling gaps at the front of a border and for edgings. Well-grown plants will sometimes flower a bit through the winter and will give the longest spring show in a cool spot on fertile soil. Don't let them self-seed, for they hybridize readily with wild daisies and so the flower quality soon deteriorates. There are some old named forms, such as the double pink 'Dresden China' or the crimson 'Rob Roy' which are obtainable from nurseries. Easy from seed and of the same small neat habit is the red, pink and white 'Pomponette Mixed'.

For Shady Beds

The polyanthus needs soil in some shade. If you raise your own from seed choose a hardier older kind, such as 'Gold Lace' or 'Old Curiosity', or a modern hybrid recommended by the seedsman for winter hardiness. Some of those with super-size blooms in bright colours are better as pot plants than for the open garden. This applies also to primroses, varieties like 'Husky Mixed' being bred for winter hardiness and outdoor flowering.

Old Favourites

The Welsh poppy (*Meconopsis cambrica*) has been grown in gardens for a long time. Once established in a garden, it will self-seed so that cheeky yellow, or occasionally orange, single flowers pop up in a delightful way among other plants.

The old double granny's bonnet columbines bred from the wild *Aquilegia vulgaris* come in such pretty soft colours that they are a must for any cottage garden. They will self-seed so that surplus young plants must be weeded out, but this is a simple matter and they don't grow strongly enough to smother other things.

It is hard to imagine an old cottage without some of the tall stems of cup-shaped flowers of the hollyhock (*Althea rosea*) against the walls. Choose from Giant Single or the old Chater's Double mixtures of seed.

The evening primrose (*Oenothera biennis*) is a self-seeder that looks a mess by day, but comes to life as dusk approaches and a new batch of big pale-yellow scented blooms opens. You can almost certainly find someone with surplus young plants to start a stock in your garden.

Grow honesty (*Lunaria annua*) for both its showy light-purple spring flowers – there is a less attractive white form – and silvery seed-case linings for autumn borders and indoor vases. Happy in shade among shrubs, it is a prolific seeder

ABOVE: *Pale yellow aquilegias, short-lived perennials which will often self-seed, grow beneath the modern shrub rose 'Constance Spry'.*

OPPOSITE: *Biennial wallflowers and forget-me-nots form a cloth through which tulips and other spring bulbs rise, forming a far lovelier picture when intermingled as here than when grown in separated batches of their own kind.*

and many young plants must be weeded out each year.

It is said that *Eryngium giganteum* is commonly called Miss Willmott's Ghost because that eccentric lady used to drop a few seeds of the plant in other people's gardens to surprise them. With prickly silvery foliage and flower heads, this sea holly does not grow very tall despite the botanical name.

Whereas early summer sowing is early enough for many biennials, put in seed of the Canterbury bell (*Campanula medium*) by mid-spring or the plants may not grow large enough to bloom the next summer. The Cup and Saucer strain in soft shades of pink, mauve, blue and white is more traditional than the dome-shaped dwarf 'Bells of Holland'.

HARDY PERENNIALS

If you plant the old-fashioned hardy border plants generously, this will give the luxuriant blend of flowers that is typical of the cottage garden style. You can raise these in different ways. Biennials and short-term perennials are usually started from seed sown in open ground in late spring; the developing plants can then be moved to flowering positions in autumn. However, longer-lived perennials are more often increased by dividing clumps of roots, though some can be raised from seed sown in pans indoors or in a frame. You can prick these seedlings out and grow them on in a nursery bed outside.

First Flowers of the Year

Long before winter is over, setterwort (*Helleborus foetidus*) opens big bunches of nodding maroon-rimmed pale-green blooms above deeply-cut dark foliage. Not so old, but ideal for a modern cottage garden are varieties of the Lenten hellebore (*Helleborus orientalis*) with its saucers of white, green, pink or purple flowers that last for ages. Grow the sweet violet (*Viola odorata*) in its most usual purple and white forms at the sunny base of a hedge or under an old fruit tree along with the common primrose (*Primula vulgaris*).

The giant catmint with Achillea 'Flowers of Sulphur' and a hybrid peony. Close blended planting of hardy perennials is one of the endearing features of cottage gardens.

The latter's double forms that date back to Tudor times need frequent division and humus-rich soil to keep them going, but there are many newer and easier primroses if you find these difficult. The simple yellow daisy blooms of doronicum are a must for the spring garden and so are the lungworts. The latter range from the old pink and blue *Pulmonaria officinalis* to the blue *Pulmonaria angustifolia azurea* and the lovely 'Sissinghurst White' which is a form of *Pulmonaria officinalis*.

The laced pink 'Gran's Favourite' takes pride of place in a mixed cottage border.

Late Spring and Early Summer

The bleeding heart (*Dicentra spectabilis*) is a real old cottage garden favourite with arching stems of deep-pink and white lockets above ferny foliage. Grow lily-of-the-valley (*Convallaria majalis*), that was once a common wild flower, at the foot of a house wall and the rich perfume of its white flowers will waft indoors. A damp spot in a bit of shade suits the fair maids of France (*Ranunculus aconitifolius* 'Flore Pleno') with pure-white double button blooms and dark divided leaves. Part shade also suits Solomon's seal (*Polygonatum multiflorum*) with arching stems of pendant green-tipped white bells, while the London pride (*Saxifraga × urbium*) with rosettes of rounded leathery leaves and stems of small pinky-white flowers will thrive in a really dull spot. The old double red cottage peony (*Paeonia officinalis* 'Rubra Plena') is thought to have been grown in gardens since Saxon times and can be left undisturbed for many years. Another old plant is the 'pretty maids all in a row' of the nursery rhyme (*Saxifraga granulata*); grow this in sun and use it to make an edging of green leaves and white blossom.

Flowers on Walls

An alpine rockery does not belong in a true cottage garden, but some of the easier dwarf plants will look comfortable growing in crevices in walls and steps. The invasive snow-in-summer (*Cerastium tomentosum*) tops mats of silvery foliage with white blossom. Golden-flowered *Alyssum saxatile* has been a garden plant for nearly three hundred years. Wee folk's stockings was one old name for *Corydalis lutea* with yellow flowers above ferny foliage. The mossy saxifrage (*Saxifraga moschata*) makes mats of evergreen foliage topped by red, pink or white bloom. The yellow self-sowing stonecrop (*Sedum acre*) will cover the flat surface of a wall and houseleeks (sempervivums) were often grown on cottage roofs to ward off lightning and fire.

Massed varieties of blue and white campanulas.

The Divine Flower

Pinks and carnations (dianthus, which means divine flower) were favourites in the old days and some varieties from long ago are well worth a place in a modern cottage garden. There is the very fragrant 'Crimson Clove' carnation; the crimson and white early nineteenth-century laced-pink 'Dad's Favourite'; the white dark-eyed 'Sops in Wine' which is said to date back to the fourteenth century; the semi-double white Tudor 'Old Fringed'; the pink-fringed-and-flecked magenta 'Allspice' and the fringed seventeenth-century 'Bridal Veil', which is a double white with a deep carmine centre. Twentieth-century breeding has introduced many new fragrant pinks with lovely colouring, healthy growth and, often, the ability to blossom continuously.

Summer Abundance

There are so many perennials to choose from for the summer display in a cottage garden. The peach-leafed bellflower (*Campanula persicifolia*) is a must with its erect stems of nodding lilac-blue or white blooms; the light-blue 'Telham Beauty' is a good variety. The cranesbills range from the sun-loving blue *Geranium pratense* and its white, purple and paler blue forms; to the shade-loving *Geranium sylvaticum* also in white or blue; and also *Geranium phaeum* which is called the mourning widow because its flowers are nearly black. The scented chrome-yellow day lily (*Hemerocallis lilio-asphodelus*) makes clumps of arching grassy leaves, will grow in sun or shade, can be left in one spot for years and, like the orange-red *Hemerocallis fulva*, has been grown for a very long time. Hattie's pincushion is an old name for *Astrantia major*; the species has pinkish-green flowers but the varieties *A. m. rosea* and *A. m. rubra* are much brighter.

Gypsophila paniculata, with its clouds of tiny white flowers, likes alkaline soil so much it has been called the chalk plant. Grow, too, the mauve meadow rue (*Thalictrum aquilegifolium*) for its pretty foliage and tall stems of fluffy blooms. The golden daisies of *Anthemis tinctoria* are good in the 'Grallagh Gold' cultivar. Neat plants with spikes of blue flowers have long made *Veronica spicata* a favourite.

Anemone × hybrida *are wonderful and reliable perennials in sun or shade and will flower into* autumn.

Last Flowers of the Year

Good for the back of a border, tall handsome *Rudbeckia laciniata* produces golden flowers with green cone centres through late summer and autumn. Japanese anemones (*Anemone × hybrida*) are ideal for a shady border where their saucers of long-stemmed pink and white blossoms appear over the same period. Sneezeweed is an old name for *Helenium autumnale* and the bronze-red 'Moorheim Beauty' is one of its best forms. The Italian starwort (*Aster amellus*) has been grown in cottage gardens longer than the Michaelmas daisies of the *novi-belgii* and *novae-angliae* types from America and the old violet-blue 'King George' cultivar is a splendid late perennial. Known as goodbye summer in the United States, *Aster lateriflorus horizontalis* carries arching stems of tiny red-centred lilac flowers into autumn. Given sun and good drainage, varieties of *Chrysanthemum rubellum* will make sturdy clumps with sprays of single flowers from late summer until the first frost and are hardy in the open ground. The pink 'Clara Curtis' and the pale yellow 'Mary Stoker' are both well-known varieties.

BULBS

There should be some colour from bulbs through much of the year in a cottage garden, though this is best provided by those that are left undisturbed in one place rather than by the kind that you lift after flowering and treat as seasonal bedding. Many bulbs that flower earliest and latest in the year can be grown around the base of fruit trees or under deciduous shrubs where there is no need for surface cultivation; their foliage can die down naturally and seed be allowed to ripen and self-sow.

ABOVE: Primrose and Crocus chrysanthus 'Skyline'.

OPPOSITE: One of the prettiest corms, Anemone nemorosa 'Allenii', under Helleborus argutifolius (syn. H. corsicus).

Winter

Small bulbs that bloom while days are short and cold are one of the first signs that spring is on the way. The first to open is usually the winter aconite (Eranthis hyemalis) which likes to grow in part-shade and, if left alone for a few years, will carpet the ground with gold flowers backed by toby-dog ruffs of green. The best way to start a patch is to dig up and move a spadeful of bulbs and soil just as the flowers are fading. That is also the best way to introduce the small snowdrop (Galanthus nivalis) to a new site. Both the single and double forms have been grown in cottage gardens for centuries and also like part-shade under a deciduous tree or shrub.

Along with these two harbingers of spring, grow the slim lavender Crocus tommasinianus and its brighter form 'Whitewell Purple' and the dumpy little Cyclamen coum in pink, deep pink and white forms which bloom at the same time. All will be happy growing in grass under a standard apple or pear tree, providing you do not give that a winter tar-oil wash. Choose full sun for varieties of Crocus chrysanthus which open early, spread freely and come in a wide range of colours often with feathery markings on the petals. Good cultivars include the softly shaded 'Blue Pearl' and the white 'Snowbunting' which has an orange throat.

Small Spring Bulbs

The little windflower (Anemone nemorosa) carpets the ground in many woods with dainty white flowers tinged pink on the outside, and sometimes there are blue, mauve or deep pink blooms. No doubt it was from the surrounding countryside that they were first moved into cottage gardens to grow in shady spots. Equally at home in this setting is the Grecian windflower (Anemone blanda) with its daisy-like blooms of blue, pink or white.

The pretty checkered Fritillaria meleagris, an old cottage garden plant, has a host of names, including lazarus bell and snake's head. It loves damp grassy places where it can be left to seed around.

Bluebells (Hyacinthoides) cluster in grass under a tree.

Larger Spring Bulbs

The crown imperial (*Fritillaria imperialis*) was mentioned by Shakespeare and has been grown in cottage gardens ever since his day. With stout stems, each topped by a cluster of drooping bells of orange-red or lemon bloom below a crown of green foliage, this will give spring colour in a mixed border before most perennial plants are sending up much growth.

Despite its common name, the summer snowflake (*Leucojum aestivum*) opens green-tipped white flowers quite early in spring and sends up bright green, straplike leaves so soon that they are often blackened by frost. Happiest on damp soil in part-shade, it can be left in one place for many years and is best grown among shrubs where its dying leaves cannot do harm by smothering nearby plants.

You could not have a cottage garden in spring without some of the narcissus family, but big bold modern varieties in bright colours are very out of place here. Instead, you need the old kinds, such as the Lent lily (*Narcissus pseudonarcissus*), with delicate golden trumpets and paler yellow petals, which naturalizes so well, and the double greenish-yellow 'Van Sion' which is said to have

bloomed first in 1620 and has an iron constitution. Both of these come early, while at the other end of the season there is the sweetly-scented old pheasant eye (*Narcissus poeticus recurvus*) with snowy swept-back petals and a tiny yellow cup edged with red. Its pure-white double form comes even later and looks a bit like a gardenia. A few weeks earlier there is the jonquil (*Narcissus jonquilla*), with up to six deep-yellow single flowers to a stem and a very rich fragrance.

Among the best tulips for a cottage garden are those with rounded oval blooms that open wide on strong wind-resistant stems, such as 'Mrs John Scheepers' which has been called the king of yellow tulips, the deep maroon 'Queen of the Night', the old and much loved pink 'Clara Butt', salmon-rose 'Palestrina', lavender-mauve 'Bleu Aimable', white and rosy-red 'Sorbet' and the marble-white 'Maureen'.

Introduced to cultivation in the mid sixteenth century, the hyacinth was common by its end and by the eighteenth century it had been learnt that bulbs were easy to force for winter blooms indoors. Wealthy people paid large sums for new and unusual varieties and it was probably the bulbs they discarded to make way for these introductions that were first grown by cottagers. Plant them under a window, by a path or near a seat where the scent of the flowers can be most enjoyed, and also in pots for the house.

Summer Bulbs

Spanish, English and Dutch irises derived from *Iris xiphium* crossed with several other bulbous species have been popular early summer flowers in sunny places on well-drained soil for a very long time and are lovely for cutting. The Dutch hybrids have the best colour range.

Believed to be the oldest domesticated flower, the Madonna lily (*Lilium candidum*) with rich yellow anthers in the centre of chalice-like pure-white blooms is happiest in a cottage garden where the soil is lime-rich and well-nourished, its roots are shaded by surrounding plants and the bulbs can be left undisturbed. The tiger lily (*Lilium lancifolium*) with tall stems of very spotted, orange recurving blooms in late summer is (like the Madonna lily), prone to virus, but also seems to grow best in a mixed cottage border.

The Dutch iris 'Golden Harvest' with blue aquilegias.

Autumn Bulbs

Colchicum autumnale, often wrongly called autumn crocus, has large bulbs, showy mauve autumn flowers, which were called naked ladies because they appeared without foliage, and large leaves which grow up in spring. It must be grown where these will be no bother, perhaps in front of a shrub.

Whereas this plant belongs to the lily family, the true autumn crocus belongs to the iris family. Dried golden stigmas of purple-flowered saffron (*Crocus sativus*) were treasured in the old days for colouring and flavouring food, for medicinal use and for making dye. *Crocus speciosus* has been in cultivation since 1800, has goblets of purple-blue bloom and is more widely grown.

The hardy pink or white *Cyclamen hederifolium* is another very pretty autumn-flowering bulb, one that was once claimed to have aphrodisiac properties. It prefers to be left alone in an undisturbed spot under a tree or in front of a shrub.

Right: *Gallica rose 'Président de Sèze'.*

Opposite: *China rose 'Old Blush China' (syn. 'Parson's Pink').*

Right: *Gallica rose 'Président de Sèze'.*

Opposite: *China rose 'Old Blush China' (syn. 'Parson's Pink').*

ROSES

Most of the old cottage garden roses were of French origin and were probably adopted by working people last century when they were thrown out by members of the gentry who were keen on the new fashion for larger and brighter hybrid blooms. Even today you can find many an old rose bush that has grown in one place, or been handed down from one garden to another, for so long that no one has a clue what it is named. The old varieties were derived from various species; almost all have a wonderful fragrance, bear much more prettily shaped flowers than modern roses and are more softly coloured.

Gallica roses are probably the oldest of all garden roses and are varieties of *Rosa gallica*, a short suckering species which is a native of Southern Europe. They are very hardy, strongly-scented and once-flowering, and make short bushy shrubs. Among them is the Apothecary's Rose, known also as the Red Rose of Lancaster (*Rosa gallica officinalis*) which dates way back into history, and its striped crimson and white sport, 'Rosa Mundi' (*Rosa gallica versicolor*).

The Damask roses are another very old group, said to have been brought from the Middle East by the Crusaders. They are less hardy and often taller than the Gallicas and have loose clusters of pink, red or white flowers which are usually richly scented. One of the most ancient varieties is 'Quatre Saisons', a clear-pink that is said to be the oldest repeat-flowering rose. Dating back to 1832, 'Madame Hardy' is a beautiful white with a suggestion of lemon in its fragrance.

Named after a Duchess of Portland who introduced a rose believed to be a hybrid between a Damask and Gallica at the end of the eighteenth century, the Portland roses were soon popular, mainly because they are repeat-flowering. They are neat enough for a small garden and one of the best is the rose-pink 'Comte de Chambord'.

Alba roses are very hardy; they make large bushes, are always white or pink, sweetly-scented, need very little care and will stand more shade than most roses. Some date back to the Middle Ages and among them is the White Rose of York, or Jacobite Rose (*Rosa alba* 'Maxima'): its creamy-white blooms open from blush-tinted buds and it can be grown as a climber. Also very old is 'Maiden's Blush', with greyish foliage, and blush-pink blooms which are richly perfumed. 'Queen of Denmark' is a strongly scented soft pink with a more deeply shaded centre and is thought by many to be one of the finest of all the old roses.

Centifolia roses, which

Portland rose 'Comte de Chambord' is compact and very recurrent.

comes from a plant found in a hedge on the Isle of Bourbon (Réunion), east of Madagascar; it was brought to France and crossed with Gallica and Damask hybrids to give a race of continuous flowering, richly scented roses with beautifully cupped flowers held on slender upright growth. These look superb trained on pillars and include such old favourites as the small white 'Boule de Neige', pink 'La Reine Victoria' and purple crimson 'Madame Isaac Pereire' that is perhaps the most heavily scented of all roses.

The ENGLISH roses, bred and introduced by David Austin, are a new race that combine the recurrent-flowering qualities and wider colour range of modern varieties with the characteristic flower formation and charm of the old ones. They are usually a little taller than a Hybrid Tea, their growth is more natural and bushy and they have a good fragrance. They look comfortable mixed with other plants, but dislike too much competition and must have room to breathe. Because they are expected to give more than one flush of bloom, these need rather more feeding than the old roses that flower only at midsummer. Among many to choose from are the rose-pink 'The Countryman', a backcross from an English rose to an old Portland, and its deeper pink sister, 'Gertrude Jekyll', which has exceptionally fragrant large flowers, shaped like rosettes.

are also known as Provence or Cabbage Roses, seem to have originated near the end of the sixteenth century from a cross between an Alba and a Damask. The very fragrant flowers are large so the bushes have a habit of hanging their heads under the weight of petals. Once-flowering, they need firm pruning to make shapely shrubs. Varieties include the lovely shell-pink 'Fantin Latour', named after the nineteenth-century painter, and the small-flowered pink 'De Meaux' which goes back to 1789. It is a shorter bush so makes a good low hedge.

MOSS roses were originally sports from Centifolias or Damasks, the first dating back to 1720. They became very popular because of their mossy growth on the flower sepals; this has a strong fragrance and makes a contrast to that of the blooms. The oldest is 'Old Pink Moss'; another desirable variety is the purple-magenta 'William Lobb', also called 'Old Velvet Moss'.

Although CHINA roses had been long cultivated in China, they did not arrive in Europe until late in the eighteenth century. Despite the drawback that they had little scent, they were soon in great demand for breeding because they flowered continuously. 'Old Blush China', also called the Monthly Rose, is reputed to be the first that arrived in Europe; in a mild season, it will bloom until mid-winter.

The name BOURBON roses

Climbers and Ramblers

Climbing roses flowering on the house walls or the porch, festooning an archway over the path or covering a trellis behind a border are an essential part of any cottage garden. The vigorous copper-pink 'Albertine', a popular large-flowered rambler, is one of the most suitable though it is too thorny to grow beside a path. It blooms for only a few weeks in midsummer when it puts up a spectacular show on a shed roof or tree. Happy in part-shade, 'Alberic Barbier' has shiny green leaves and creamy flowers opening from yellow buds that come mainly at midsummer. Semi-evergreen 'Félicité et Perpétue' has large clusters of small creamy rosettes with a delicate scent and is vigorous enough to go over a small tree. Clear-pink 'Dorothy Perkins' is very free-flowering and has been highly popular, but it is one of those ramblers that need all its old-flowered stems cut to the ground in late summer and is very prone to mildew. 'New Dawn' is little more than sixty years old, but is a most valuable climber with shapely blush-pink blooms which continue over a long period. The summer-flowering pink rose 'Constance Spry', though usually grown as a shrub, can make a glorious climber.

How to Grow Roses

Old roses are not plants for formal rose beds, but are more at home in a border among herbaceous plants, perhaps edged with lavender or old-fashioned pinks. Choose mostly plants that flower before or after the midsummer rose show to ensure a long season of colour. Some old roses make very large bushes, so choose those of compact habit for a small garden, or train taller ones over tripods made from rustic timber, or against pillars.

Modern 'old-style' rose 'Magenta' among campanulas and astrantias.

Clematis can scramble comfortably among the branches of the climbing rose 'New Dawn'.

CLIMBERS

Climbing plants growing luxuriantly against the walls, over the porch, outbuildings, arbours and archways are the hallmark of the cottage garden. Many popular varieties in the old days were chosen for fragrance as much as for beauty and when planted by a seat or on house walls their scent could be enjoyed even when flowers were out of sight. Roses were universal favourites and climbing varieties have been included on the previous pages.

Perhaps the most popular of all other climbers was honeysuckle (*Lonicera periclymenum*), which was probably first brought into cottage gardens from the surrounding countryside. Happiest where its roots are shaded by other plants, but its twining stems can grow up to open richly-perfumed flowers in sun, it is an easy choice for growing over a porch, archway, or fence and can be allowed to go up through an old tree. Early Dutch ('Belgica') and Late Dutch ('Serotina') are the best-known varieties.

The summer-flowering common jasmine (*Jasminum officinale*) has been grown in gardens for centuries and is superb for clambering over and screening an ugly

Lathyrus latifolius is an old cottage-garden climbing perennial.

Modern large-flowered hybrid clematis cut back hard every year don't blend into a cottage garden very well, but you could grow the rich purple *Clematis jackmanii* and allow it to ramble through a tree to give a mass of the smaller blooms that result from little pruning. *Clematis montana* does suit the style well and can be allowed to scramble over the room of a garage or large shed, or will transform an ugly chain link fence into a thing of beauty. The strong-growing and sweetly-scented *Clematis flammula* is a much older garden plant with a mass of small starry white flowers in late summer. It is good on a high fence or, when pruned hard in late winter, ideal for growing through a lilac or another shrub that is dull after its spring flowers are over.

Native to the Eastern U.S.A., Virginia creeper (*Parthenocissus quinque-folia*) has long been grown in cottage gardens as a self-clinging vine whose leaves colour richly in early autumn. It will go up over a cottage roof or hide the ugliest shed.

The everlasting pea (*Lathyrus latifolius*) has no scent, but is an easy perennial which dies right down in autumn then sends up new stems in spring which will go up over a hedge or bush and open long-stemmed clusters of rosy-mauve or white flowers for many weeks of summer.

outbuilding. Its trusses of small white flowers from midsummer on are very sweetly scented. The starry yellow flowers of winter jasmine (*Jasminum nudiflorum*) are borne on bare twigs in milder spells from leaf fall until late winter and have no scent. Not nearly such a vigorous plant, this is good on a shady wall or where it can cascade down a bank, and it looks lovely growing through the fish-

bone-style branches of *Cotoneaster horizontalis* with its red berries and leaves which colour well before falling.

With its long racemes of fragrant mauve bloom just as the leaves are unfurling in late spring, *Wisteria sinensis* has long been a favourite climber. It must have a sunny position and will cover quite a large area of wall or roof. It is superb, too, for growing on a rustic frame over a seat to form an arbour.

49

ABOVE: Floor of Geranium endressii beneath a magnolia.
RIGHT: Simple topiary ball surrounded by delphiniums and foxgloves.

TREES AND SHRUBS

In a closely-planted cottage garden there is little room for ornamental trees and shrubs. In fact shrubs that have been grown for a very long time tend to be quite small and neat like *Daphne mezereum*, whose bare branches are wreathed in rosy-mauve scented flowers in late winter followed by poisonous red fruits at midsummer. Others are happy pruned hard to make wall shrubs like the japonica (chaenomeles), whose flowers open on bare branches early in spring.

The common myrtle (*Myrtus communis*) is best grown near a warm wall and in the old days was often grown from a sprig taken out of a bridal bouquet. Its aromatic foliage is evergreen, but liable to be browned by frost, and its small white summer flowers are followed by purple-black berries in a warm year.

Box (*Buxus sempervirens*) in both its green and variegated forms is also easy from cuttings and was often clipped by cottagers into neat balls or simple topiary shapes. The scent from the small evergreen leaves is evocative of old-world gardens. A clipped yew (*Taxus baccata*) trained into a topiary shape might form the centre of a flower bed in the front garden, its dark evergreen foliage contrasting well with the abundant blooms growing nearby.

A holly tree (*Ilex aquifolium*) found in an old cottage garden may have been planted there by a former owner or have grown from a seed dropped by a bird. Slow-growing and adaptable to different soils and situations, this cannot be bettered for a winter show of foliage and fruit.

The laurustinus (*Viburnum tinus*) has been grown for several hundred years and has dark glossy evergreen leaves; its flat heads of white bloom opening from pink-tinged buds from autumn until spring make it a most valuable shrub.

A number of shrubs provide spring colour for a cottage garden. These include the flowering currant (*Ribes sanguineum*) with dropping racemes of rosy-pink bloom; the rich golden Jew's mallow (*Kerria japonica*)

best-known in its double form, and the mauve common lilac (*Syringa vulgaris*) and its many cultivars. When space permits more than just a fruit tree, there is the laburnum with long racemes of yellow bloom, or a double red or pink form of hawthorn such as *Crataegus laevigata* (syn. *C. oxyacantha*) 'Rosea Flore Pleno'.

Also suggested for hedges, the old English lavender (*Lavandula angustifolia*) can make quite a wide-spreading bush of aromatic silver foliage topped by spikes of purple bloom that are loved by bees and butterflies. Used for hedging in mild areas and fine as a free-standing bush, *Fuchsia magellanica* has long slender scarlet and violet flowers on stems that may be cut to the ground in winter. Hydrangea bushes with large mophead blooms opening cream then turning to pale pink or blue grow in shady corners of many a cottage garden; the old variety 'Joseph Banks' was introduced from China late in the eighteenth century.

The rowan (*Sorbus aucuparia*) was a tree often planted outside houses to ward off witches and the red early autumn berries had various culinary uses.

The barberry (*Berberis vulgaris*) makes a spiny bush with clusters of yellow spring flowers, then red autumn fruits and foliage. In bygone days this had many household uses, but most people today will prefer to grow the neater *Berberis wilsoniae* or *Berberis* 'Rubrostilla'.

HERBS

Herbs have been grown in cottage gardens longer than any other plants. Expensive imported spices flavoured the rich man's food, but the poor relied on home-grown herbs to improve the taste of a monotonous diet with meat that was often far from fresh. Housewives in the past grew herbs for medicinal use as well as for their fragrance: they used the plants to strew on floors, keep away clothes moths and other pests, scent linen, make toilet water and cosmetics or to dye wool and other cloth.

Today herbs are back in favour for culinary use, and their lovely scents are enjoyed whether in the garden or dried in potpourris and herbal sachets. The plants can be grown in a special herb bed, used to line a path and partially hide the vegetable plot, or mingled among perennials in the flower borders.

Parsley (*Petroselinum crispum*) needs to be freshly sown each year and, because it likes a fertile soil, is often grown among vegetables.

The rich green curly leaves are decorative and look attractive when the herb is sown in a patch near a path where plants can be watered in dry weather and easily gathered on wet days.

The pot marigold (*Calendula officinalis*) is a cheery annual that lends itself to being grown among foliage herbs; if its flowers are allowed to go to seed, it will self-sow and save you work next year. Start with a good variety such as 'Orange King Improved' and allow only good flowers to seed.

Quick-growing chervil *Anthriscus cerefolium*), with aniseed-flavoured ferny leaves that are good in a salad, is an easy annual which will seed around. Another is borage (*Borago officinalis*) with blue flowers beloved by bees and rough leaves tasting of cucumber.

Feverfew (*Chrysanthemum parthenium*) is best treated as an annual and once established in the garden will seed around all over the place. Often recommended nowadays as a cure for migraine, the species deserves a place for its pretty aromatic divided leaves and branching stems of single white daisy blooms. Grow, too, the golden-leafed form and that with double white flowers.

Bergamot, Monarda didyma, (right) is worthy of a place in the perennial border.

Golden marjoram, Origanum vulgare aureum, *lights up a herb bed.*

Richer Cooler Soils

Chives (*Allium schoenoprasum*) have been grown for centuries and are indispensable in a modern cottage garden for their grassy leaves of mild onion flavour and mauve thrift-like flowers. Good for edgings, the plants like a fertile soil in some shade and need to be lifted and split up every couple of years. There is also a more decorative giant form, *A.s. sibiricum*.

Lovage (*Levisticum officinale*) prefers cool rich soil where, each spring, it produces large leaves strongly flavoured of celery and tall stems topped by umbels of yellow-green summer bloom. It is a handsome plant and its leaves are splendid for flavouring chicken, soups and stews.

Lemon balm (*Melissa officinalis*) may self-seed too freely, but is an essential perennial in the cottage garden, and grown since ancient times by bee keepers because the insignificant white flowers are so popular with the insects. Various old records claim that people have attributed their very long life to regularly drinking tea which is made from the leaves.

Bee balm and sweet bergamot are two names for the North American *Monarda didyma* which was used to make a tea by the Oswego Indians. A herb for rich moist but light soil, its whorls of red, pink, mauve, or purple shaggy blooms topping stems of scented leaves make it worthy of a place in the perennial border.

The Mints

There are many kinds of mint and all have the same running roots that spread rapidly. The solution is to confine plants by growing them in an old bath or other bottomless metal container sunk nearly to the rim in the ground – leave a couple of inches above or the roots will run out over the top. Alternatively dig mint up and replant it every year before the roots have time to spread too far. Spearmint (*Mentha spicata*) is the most popular, but peppermint, apple, ginger and eau-de-cologne mints are worth growing also.

Sun-lovers

A sunny dry spot on poor soil, a narrow bed near a warm wall, a steep bank, or place where a few bricks or stones have been left out of a paved area, are all good homes for the many aromatic herbs that are natives of the warm lands of southern Europe. Here you can grow common and lemon thymes (*Thymus vulgaris* and *Thymus × citriodorus*) and their varieties that have so many uses in the kitchen and make very low bushy plants with evergreen foliage and pretty mauve blooms at midsummer.

The oregano used in Mediterranean cookery – the marjoram (*Origanum vulgare*) – is a showy perennial with rosy-mauve flowers that attract butterflies and bees to the garden. Pot marjoram (*Origanum onites*) is also much used in cookery, but this is rather less attractive.

The grey-green leaves of the common sage (*Salvia officinalis*) have been used for centuries for cooking with goose, pork and other rich meats and were eaten as a spring tonic to purify the blood and give long life. A bushy evergreen, easy from cuttings, it likes dry soil and sun and has spikes of purple-blue midsummer bloom worthy of a place in a flower border.

ABOVE: *A mound of* Artemisia abrotanum *(centre)*.

LEFT: *The golden umbels of the plumy-leafed fennel,* Foeniculum vulgare, *in a border with the pink physostegia and acanthus.*

Rue (*Ruta graveolens*) was an important strewing herb in the old days, but is mainly grown today for the pretty divided and very aromatic leaves that are best in the 'Jackman's Blue' form.

Cotton lavender (*Santolina chamaecyparissus*) used to be grown as an insect repellent and if you are troubled by clothes moths try placing some branches in drawers and wardrobes or under carpets. Its silvery filigree foliage is topped by golden button blooms and a row of bushes can make a good mini-hedge. For contrast grow the bright green shrub *Santolina rosmarinifolia*.

Common fennel (*Foeniculum vulgare*) is a tall perennial with feathery leaves and big umbels of yellowish summer bloom which will self-seed in both its green and bronze forms. Both seeds and leaves are good in fish dishes.

Taller Shrubs

Rosemary (*Rosmarinus officinalis*) is a must for every cottage garden and sited in a hot dry spot near a path or the door will give off a rich aroma every time the narrow grey-green leaves are brushed in passing. Its evergreen foliage can be used in cooking all the year round and the blue blooms will attract bees.

The sweet bay (*Laurus nobilis*) can be grown in a container, or in a warm sheltered place in the open where it will grow into an evergreen tree; its leaves may be blackened by frost in severe winters, but branches will invariably re-shoot.

Southernwood and lad's love are old names for *Artemisia abrotanum* from South Europe that revels in a hot dry position and makes a shrubby plant with feathery grey-green leaves whose scent is richest after a shower of rain or when bruised.

Nasturtiums climb among espaliered apple trees.

In old cottage gardens apples were usually grown on tall standard or half-standard trees; their height meant that it was more difficult to pick the fruit from these than from modern bush trees, but it allowed gooseberries or shade-loving flowers to grow under the branches. If you are planting an apple tree in a small plot, choose a family tree where two or three compatible varieties have been grafted onto one stock, or grow several espaliers or a row of cordons to divide one part of the garden from another. If there are other apples in nearby gardens to act as pollinators, a tree of the Bramley Seedling cooker gives very good value with pretty pink and white blossom and a crop that stores well.

Soft Fruit

Blackberries or logan-berries can be trained on fences or on rustic archways over a path if thornless varieties are chosen. A row of raspberry canes can make a screen to hide the compost heap, gooseberries take up little room if grown as cordons and a few blackcurrant bushes on one side of a path can be underplanted with pansies or primroses for early colour. Strawberries need little space, give a quicker harvest than any fruit and are worth the care they need to protect fruit from pests and diseases. Alpine varieties are usually trouble-free.

FRUIT AND VEGETABLES

It is hard to imagine a real cottage garden without any culinary crops and, with careful planning, some of the most important can be blended so skilfully into a plot overflowing with flowers that they add to its decorative appearance.

Top Fruit

A Morello cooking-cherry trained as a fan on a shady wall looks pleasing when hung with white spring blossom and later with dark-red summer fruit. In contrast, choose a sunny wall for a gage, dessert plum or pear. A pear will go up to the eaves if grown against the side of a two-storey house and is lovely covered in white bloom and with golden fruit in autumn.

A sensible and productive working vegetable garden, complete with compost heap and bin.

Vegetables

There have been many changes in the selection of vegetables eaten by most households in the past quarter of a century and it could be argued that the cottage garden should include only those that date back into the past. But, whereas most cottagers aimed at self-sufficiency and growing enough potatoes, onions and cabbages to last all the year, the modern gardener doesn't like to grow them, but concentrates on crops that are expensive to buy, not readily available in the shops or are best eaten very soon after harvesting. Most people now also prefer to grow small groups of a lot of attractive vegetables rather than boring long rows of staple crops.

Roots

Cottagers have always grown a lot of roots, and a part of the plot that has not been manured in the current winter should be reserved for parsnips, early and maincrop carrots, beetroot and swedes. The old long beet stores well for winter eating, but a bolt-resistant globe variety is best for early spring sowing. Early Nantes type carrots can be sown then, but early summer is soon enough for the maincrop which you lift in autumn and store in boxes of sand through winter. Parsnips from a spring sowing can be left in the ground to be dug as needed through winter. Swedes are sown in late spring to lift as required in the cold months. Maincrop potatoes are not worth growing in a small plot, but a short row of a first early variety will give delicious new tubers with a far superior flavour to those that you could buy from a shop.

Ready for autumn; lifted potatoes and brassica in a garden edged with pinks and nicotiana.

Brassicas

The most important members of the cabbage family are those seldom seen in good condition in the shops such as purple sprouting broccoli which you harvest in early spring following a late spring sowing the previous year, or dwarf curly kale which is a good-looking and very hardy cut-and-come-again winter brassica. If you have space, the Brussels sprout is an old favourite that is well worth including.

Legumes

A truly decorative vegetable, the scarlet runner bean trained up rustic poles, canes or netting and stakes can make a productive summer screen. Sow it in two or three batches on fertile soil and water it in dry spells to ensure long slim pods over several months.

Broad beans have been grown for far longer than runner beans. In milder areas the hardiest longpod varieties can be sown in autumn for midsummer picking. However,

where space for vegetables is limited, and you wish to grow peas, give preference to early marrowfat varieties which are ready to pick at midsummer and can be cleared to make way for a follow-on crop. This could be a row of hardy leeks that have been grown for centuries, or either Swiss chard or spinach beet which will produce leaves you can gather over many months.

Salads

Tomatoes are a comparatively new crop and do best outdoors when planted near a sunny wall, ideally with some protection for the first three or four weeks after a late spring planting. Modern outdoor cucumbers bear fruits that compare well in quality with greenhouse varieties if trained up a tripod of rustic sticks to allow developing fruit to hang down and grow straight. Again, plant them out in late spring and give protection for a while. Sow a short row of lettuce every few weeks from early spring to mid-summer, using butterhead, crisphead, cos and loose leaf types, then put in a hardy variety in early

A line of sweet peas is always a charming addition to the cottage vegetable garden.

autumn to overwinter for spring cutting. A few radish seeds sown among slower growing vegetables every month through the growing season give a supply of tender juicy roots.

Miscellany

Sweet corn is a modern vegetable that looks handsome grown in a block to assist pollination and give a good harvest. The site of last year's compost heap is ideal for the marrow plants grown in most old gardens, or the courgettes that are preferred today. Smaller and milder than onions, shallots have been cultivated for a great many years, take up little space and need little care. Save some

from each harvest for next year's planting.

That is what you do also with the Jerusalem artichoke, a relative of the sunflower with knobbly tubers that make good winter soup. Grow a row at the end of the garden to give a summer screen of tall stems and lift them in the dormant season for the kitchen.

A part-shaded corner on good humus-rich soil is a suitable place for rhubarb, which is truly a vegetable though eaten as a fruit. It can be forced if covered with a wooden box.

Asparagus has been grown in gardens for several hundred years and after a very few years a bed of a modern variety will give many succulent spears for late spring eating. Its ferny summer foliage is a pretty companion in a vase with sweet peas and other cut flowers.

ABOVE: *Ali-baba terracotta jar of sempervivums.*

RIGHT: *Trough of pansies with nigella seed-heads in the foreground.*

CONTAINERS

The tradition for indoor windowsills of cottages to be tightly packed with pot plants dates back to the time when almost all the space in the garden had to be devoted to food crops and herbs. Rooms already very poorly lit because windows were small and ceilings low with dark beams were made even darker by the forest of growth from plants that often grew halfway up the glass. Few ornamentals could be grown outside, but here the house-wife could lovingly tend plants grown purely for pleasure.

Geraniums (pelargoniums) were favourites. *Pelargonium crispum variegatum* with small cream and green crinkled foliage and the vigorous lemon-scented *P.*

graveolens, both dating back to 1774, were two of those grown for scented foliage. The famous scarlet 'Paul Crampel', salmon-pink 'King of Denmark' and double 'Apple Blossom Rosebud' are three popular Victorian varieties grown for their flowers.

The Christmas cactus (*Schlumbergera truncata*) with flat succulent stems and hanging magenta-pink flowers in autumn and winter and the rat's tail cactus (*Aporocactus flagelliformis*) with long hairy and rather ugly stems and cerise spring flowers are among the old house plants which are still popular today.

Among foliage plants that have long been loved by cottagers are the piggy-back plant (*Tolmiea menziesii*) which forms tiny plantlets at the base of the mature leaves; mother of thousands (*Saxi-fraga sarmentosa*) which produces tiny plants at the end of long thread-like stems,

maidenhair fern (*Adiantum capillus-veneris*) with dainty much-divided fronds and mind - your - own - business (*Helxine soleirolii*) which forms a carpet of tiny leaves.

In the Garden

Cottage garden plants are better grown in the open ground where possible, but may go in containers at the base of walls or in a backyard where soil cannot be dug to make a bed. Stone troughs or

large clay pots filled to the brim with flowers and foliage add charm to the front of a cottage whose door opens onto the street. Window boxes may be used here, but care must be taken that the contents do not compete with pot plants growing inside.

Though half-hardy annuals and other seasonal bedding are not in character with this style of gardening, wall-flowers and tulips or sweet-scented hyacinths and double daisies are fine for spring. Geraniums (pelar-goniums), probably raised from cuttings from indoor plants, are good for sunny spots, or ferns for shady ones, through summer.

Containers need to blend naturally into their surroundings in a cottage garden and an old stone sink or chimney pot, a wooden half barrel or animal feeding trough will do so more readily than new terracotta, while plastic or imitation antique metal seldom looks right.

Almost any plant that will grow in the open garden can be grown in a container, but those that need sharp drainage are especially suitable. Herbs grow and look decorative in pots, and a rosemary or bay is excellently placed near the kitchen door, as is a trough of mixed perennial herbs. Sedums and sempervivums are superb for shallow sinks, and so are less invasive alpines. The lining of an old copper, or a half barrel, will allow climbing plants to be grown against walls if there is no soil in which to plant them.

INDEX